# AN APPROACH TO GREEK SCULPTURE

# AN APPROACH TO GREEK SCULPTURE

BY

A. J. B. WACE, M.A., Hon. Litt.D.

*Laurence Professor of Classical Archaeology and Fellow of Pembroke College in the University of Cambridge*

AN INAUGURAL LECTURE
DELIVERED BEFORE THE UNIVERSITY
ON 17 MAY
1935

CAMBRIDGE
AT THE UNIVERSITY PRESS
1935

CAMBRIDGE
UNIVERSITY PRESS

University Printing House, Cambridge CB2 8BS, United Kingdom

Published in the United States of America by Cambridge University Press, New York

Cambridge University Press is part of the University of Cambridge.

It furthers the University's mission by disseminating knowledge in the pursuit of education, learning and research at the highest international levels of excellence.

www.cambridge.org
Information on this title: www.cambridge.org/9781107672123



First published 1935
Re-issued 2014

*A catalogue record for this publication is available from the British Library*

ISBN 978-1-107-67212-3 Paperback

## PREFATORY NOTE

SOME of the substance of this lecture was contained in a paper read to the Society for the Promotion of Hellenic Studies in 1931. The first draft of that paper was already roughed out when I read Kluge's important article 'Die Gestaltung des Erzes in der archaisch-griechischen Kunst' (*J.d.I.* 1929, p. 1 ff.). My debt to him is great. I am also most grateful for kind criticism and advice from several friends, Professors Ashmole, Beazley, Lehmann-Hartleben, and Snijder, Miss Gisela Richter, and Mr Richard Bedford, but the responsibility for the following is entirely my own.

# AN APPROACH TO GREEK SCULPTURE

THE term Sculpture in modern usage generally comprehends three arts: carving in stone or marble, bronze casting, modelling in clay or some similar material. These are in actual fact three different artistic processes, although models in some material are an essential antecedent for bronze casting. That ancient critics distinguished these three arts from one another and also from a fourth art, metal chasing, is quite clear from Pliny's treatment of them in his *Natural History*. If further proof were needed it can be seen in the remark attributed to Pasiteles,[1] that modelling was the mother of chasing, bronze casting, and marble carving. Pliny's treatment of these three processes as separate was presumably not his own, but derived from the authorities from whom he made his compilation. Thus it seems certain

[1] Pliny, *N.H.* xxxv, 156.

that this distinction among the four sculptural arts goes back at least to Xenokrates,[1] an artist and art critic of the third century B.C. Duris of Samos in the fourth century and Antigonos of Karystos in the third also treated chasing as a separate art. The importance of chasing lay in its use for the making of gold and ivory statues and for finishing statues cast in bronze. Thus we are told that Pheidias was the first to show the great possibilities of metal chasing and that Polykleitos followed in his footsteps.[2] This presumably refers to their work on the famous gold and ivory statues at Athens, Olympia, and the Heraion of Argos. Both were noted for their statues in bronze, and in this respect, as chasers and as workers in bronze, may be compared with Benvenuto Cellini. Many of the references[3] by ancient authors to

[1] See Schweitzer, 'Xenokrates von Athen' (*Schriften d. Königsberger Gelehrten Gesellschaft*, IX, 1932, p. I ff.).

[2] Pliny, *N.H.* XXXIV, 54, 55. *Toreutice* in these passages is often (e.g. by Jex-Blake and Sellers) mistranslated as 'sculpture'.

[3] E.g. Overbeck, *Schriftquellen*, 775–779; cf. Pliny, *N.H.* XXXVI, 18, *adeo momenta omnia capacia artis illi fuere.*

Pheidias refer to the beauty of his chasing. Thus Pheidias was presumably only a sculptor in the broadest modern sense of that word, but this point must be considered later.

Under the modern use of the word sculpture most writers on Greek sculpture have hitherto treated works in bronze, in stone or marble, and in clay as of equal value for the purposes of artistic comparison and for obtaining some conception of the style of an artist or of a school. It seems to be tacitly assumed that a school or an artist could work alike in any one of these materials and in metal chasing as well. The practice of sculptors in more recent times has added to this confusion because usually an artist has modelled his figure in clay from which casts could be taken. Thus the figure could be reproduced equally well in bronze by casting by professional founders, or in marble by pointing off by professional stone carvers. There is then no certainty that a finished bronze or marble figure by some well-known artist, Rodin for instance, was ever actually worked on by the master himself. In many cases it is only too clear that the artist made only the clay model and that the rest was left to workmen.

The ancients, however, distinguished between the various crafts which combined to produce a work of art. Just as an Attic vase will be found signed[1] Ἐργότιμος ἐποίησεν, Κλιτίας ἔγραψεν, so several statue bases found in Rhodes bear the name of the artist and of the caster, as for instance[2] Διοπείθης Ἀργεῖος ἐποίησε, Ἰατροκλῆς Πασικρίτου ἐχαλκούργησε. So too a bronze by Rodin bears his signature and also the name of a Paris firm of bronze founders.

If the Greeks so distinguished the four arts ought we not to do so to-day in our attempts to estimate the style of the ancient artists who were renowned in them? Can we any longer treat cast bronze, stone or marble, modelled clay, and chased metal as interchangeable materials? Is it fair, for instance, to contrast

[1] Furtwängler-Reichhold, I, pls. 1–3.

[2] Kinch, *Exploration Archéologique de Rhodes*, IV, p. 23 ff.; *Clara Rhodos*, II, p. 199, No. 31, cf. *ibid.* VI–VII, p. 403, No. 30, l. 34; *I.G.* XII, l. 106.

the Delian Diadumenos, a Hellenistic copy in marble after Polykleitos' bronze, with a statue carved direct in marble like the Kouros in New York? Although some artists, Michelangelo for instance, have excelled in more than one medium, as a rule, however, an artist is happier in one particular medium than in any other. We should therefore compare bronze or copies of bronzes with bronzes, marble with marble, and so on. Thus in Greek sculpture we ought to treat the four arts separately and should not put the archaic kouroi in stone or marble into the same category as the innumerable marble copies after Polykleitos' bronze athletes. That this can suggest a fresh approach for the study of ancient art is shown by the influence of some sculptors of to-day, Eric Gill, Henry Moore, John Skeaping, Barbara Hepworth, Richard Bedford, who work direct in stone or marble and have wisely and of set purpose abandoned the traditional sculptor's practice of employing workmen to point off a statue from a model in clay. The rise of modern sculptors of this type has opened our eyes to a fresh appreciation of archaic Greek art, especially the early figures carved direct in stone or marble, like those from Branchidai in the British Museum or the kouroi from the sanctuary of Apollo Ptoios.

The distinction between works cast in bronze after models in wood, clay or plaster and works carved direct from stone or marble is no new idea. Brunn [1] long ago in 1883 and 1884 called attention to the importance of this and quoted the well-known passage of Michelangelo [2] defining the difference between carving and modelling, and himself made some very apt remarks on the subject especially in connection with archaic sculpture in marble. Löwy in his *Rendering of Nature in Greek Art* was clearly aware of it and in a later paper [3] has emphasised the technical difference between these two artistic processes. E. Kjellberg,[4] too, was con-

[1] *Kleine Schriften*, II, p. 99 ff.

[2] Letter CDLXII: *Io intendo scultura, quella che si fa per forza di levare: quella che si fa per via di porre, è simile alla pittura.*

[3] 'Stein und Erz in der statuarischen Kunst' (*Kunstgeschichtliche Anzeigen*, 1913).

[4] *Studien zu den attischen Reliefs des V Jahrhunderts* (especially chapter IV).

scious of the distinction and rightly comments on the plastic character of bronze dependent on its preliminary models in clay or wax in contradistinction to marble. Most works also of an encyclopaedic nature, like that of Daremberg and Saglio, rightly and properly treat the four artistic processes, carving, bronze casting, modelling, and metal chasing, as separate. Still, however, apparently no historian of ancient sculpture has yet attempted to follow up this line of approach to its logical consequences. Let us therefore attempt to do so and examine some of the considerations which arise.

Pliny remarked that the carving of marble appeared as an art to be older than that of bronze casting.[1] The first sculptors in marble whom he mentions are Dipoinos and Skyllis who flourished in the fiftieth Olympiad, 580–577 B.C. They are said to have migrated from Crete to the Peloponnese and the style of their school, it is believed, can be recognised in some monuments which exist. Before their time, however, an independent school of marble

[1] *N.H.* xxxv, 153.

sculpture seems to have existed in the islands. This can be traced back to Mikkiades of Chios, who was followed by his son Archermos and his grandsons Bupalos and Athenis who flourished in the sixtieth Olympiad, 540–537 B.C.[1] They worked in Parian marble. We may regard these artists as representative of the nameless sculptors who created the archaic kouroi and korai which mostly date from the sixth century, though some date back to the late seventh century. There seems to have been a tradition that marble sculpture flourished in archaic times, and of this the surviving monuments give ample confirmation.

The next sculptor in marble mentioned by Pliny is Pheidias, which seems to suggest that from the close of the sixth century to the middle of the fifth century, during a period when famous artists in bronze were common,

[1] Pliny, whose account is confused (see Jex-Blake and Sellers, *The Elder Pliny's Chapters on the History of Art*, p. 186), mistakes the hero Melas for the father of Mikkiades, gives sixty years to a generation, and so by counting backwards conveniently makes the beginning of sculpture coincide with the first Olympiad.

there was no marble sculptor in Greece recorded by his authorities. As to Pheidias, Pliny[1] says that he is said to have worked in marble and mentions an Aphrodite in the gallery of Octavia attributed to him. This might not necessarily have been an original, but, in the light of what we now know about copies after works by famous artists of the fifth century,[2] might well have been a marble *after* and not *by* Pheidias. Pliny[3] then mentions Alkamenes and Agorakritos as pupils of Pheidias. It is not clear whether they are here mentioned as sculptors in marble or as pupils of Pheidias. Bronze works by both are recorded and Alkamenes worked the gold and ivory Dionysos at Athens. Pliny also refers to the story of the competition between them and

[1] *N.H.* xxxvi, 15.

[2] E.g. the Stockholm copy of the Agorakritos basis (Kjellberg, *op. cit.* pl. vii), the fragmentary copy in New York of the Eleusis relief (Richter, *Sculpture and Sculptors*, fig. 481), the Madrid puteal copying the east pediment of the Parthenon (*Hesperia*, II, p. 44, fig. 9), and the imitations of the Nike temple balustrade in Munich and Rome (Richter, *op. cit.* figs. 505, 507).

[3] *N.H.* xxxvi, 17 ff.

this must be examined later. Pliny next proceeds straight to Praxiteles, *marmore clarior atque ideo felicior, qui marmoris gloria superavit etiam semet.* Here, too, are mentioned Praxiteles' contemporaries, Skopas, Bryaxis, and Timotheos, as being also workers in marble, and after that comes a host of lesser names of Hellenistic and Graeco-Roman times among whom Pasiteles and Stephanos alone need be noted. These latter we know were modellers. The only famous bronze statuary who is mentioned as having worked also in marble is Kanachos,[1] *invenio et Canachum laudatum inter statuarios fecisse marmorea.* This is perfectly possible, but as the remark immediately succeeds a long passage devoted to Roman galleries of marble sculptures it is equally probable that this note of Pliny's refers rather to a marble copy in Rome of some bronze by Kanachos.

As regards sculpture in bronze, Pliny's statement[2] *innumera prope artificum multitudo nobili-*

[1] Pliny, *N.H.* xxxvi, 41.

[2] *Ibid.* xxxiv, 49.

*tata est* as regards the late sixth, the fifth, and the early fourth century is entirely confirmed by the records. The long list of masters who worked in bronze given by Pliny alone is most striking. They begin with Antenor, the artist of the first group of the Tyrannicides set up about 506 B.C.,[1] and run down to Lysippos. This first group of the Tyrannicides made before the end of the sixth century, which was carried off to Persia by Xerxes[2] and subsequently returned by Alexander or one of the Diadochi, must presumably have been hollow cast, for if solid cast it would have been difficult to transport and also too expensive to make. The mere existence of such a group before the end of the sixth century suggests that by that time the art of hollow casting life-sized figures in bronze was well established in Greece. Small solid cast bronzes of the seventh and sixth cen-

[1] Overbeck, *Schriftquellen*, 443–447.

[2] There is no reason to distrust the story that Xerxes carried this bronze group off to Persia. The French have found at Susa a solid cast bronze knuckle bone, made by Isikles (*Rev. Études Grecques*, 1921, p. 64 ff.). It is probably part of the spoils of Miletus, for it had been dedicated to Apollo.

turies are comparatively common, but hollow cast bronzes are distinctly rare. The earliest hollow cast bronzes, the head in Karlsruhe[1] and the head in Boston,[2] said to be from Sparta, are small, and with them can be grouped the griffin heads which adorned bronze cauldrons.[3] The earlier griffin heads are of hammered bronze plate made probably on a wooden model.[4] Only the later griffin heads are cast hollow, but these again are small. The earliest hollow cast bronzes of any size, the Poseidon from Livadostro,[5] the bronze Zeus head from Olympia,[6] the bearded head from the Acropolis,[7] all date towards the end of the sixth century. This was the age of Antenor and

[1] *Antike Plastik*, p. 245 ff., pl. 20.

[2] Furtwängler, *Kleine Schriften*, II, p. 429 ff., pl. 44; Langlotz, *Frühgriechische Bildhauerschulen*, pl. 53.

[3] Lamb, *Greek and Roman Bronzes*, p. 70 ff. The excavations at Samos and Perachora have yielded many more, but they are not yet published.

[4] The process is described by Furtwängler, *Olympia*, IV, p. 119. Compare the bronze from Samos, Buschor, *Altsamische Standbilder*, II, figs. 74, 77.

[5] 'Εφ. 'Αρχ. 1899, pls. 5, 6.

[6] *Olympia*, IV, pl. 1.

[7] 'Εφ. 'Αρχ. 1887, pl. 3; Langlotz, *op. cit.* p. 99.

several other artists who worked in bronze, Kanachos, Ageladas, and Onatas. It would thus seem that once the art of hollow casting large figures in bronze had been introduced the Greeks rapidly became expert and were soon able to cast such figures easily. After the Persian War we have, to mention existing bronzes, the Delphic Charioteer, the Chatsworth head,[1] and the Zeus from Artemisium,[2] and with these we can class the second group of the Tyrannicides by Kritios and Nesiotes, erected 477–476 B.C.[3]

Ancient tradition[4] reported by Pausanias gives to Rhoikos and Theodoros of Samos the credit of having been the first to cast bronze statues. Diodorus indicates that they spent some time in Egypt apparently in connection with their art as bronze founders. This is quite conceivably true and it is interesting that the name Rhoikos appears among those of the dedicators at the shrine of Aphrodite at Nau-

[1] *Ant. Denkmäler*, IV, pls. 21–23.

[2] Ἀρχ. Δελτ. XIII, pls. 1–5.

[3] Richter, *op. cit.* p. 197 f.

[4] Overbeck, *Schriftquellen*, 277–279.

kratis[1] though it is, of course, impossible to say whether the artist and the dedicator were the same person. Kluge[2] shows that the earliest Greek bronze statues we possess were cast in sections, apparently from wooden models, and afterwards fitted together much in the way in which the Foundry Vase in Berlin[3] shows bronze statues being fitted together. He shows that this method of casting bronze could have evolved naturally from the earlier method of covering wooden figures with plates of hammered bronze. Such was the statue of Zeus by Klearchos of Rhegion seen at Sparta by Pausanias[4] and said to be the oldest bronze statue known. It is also interesting that the two oldest athlete statues at Olympia of Praxidamas (544 B.C.) and Rhexibios (536 B.C.) are said by Pausanias[5] to have been of wood. Further, there was in the temple of Apollo Ismenios at Thebes a cedar wood replica of the bronze

[1] Gardner, *Naukratis*, II, p. 65, No. 778.
[2] *J.d.I.* 1929, p. 1 ff.
[3] Furtwängler-Reichhold, III, pl. 135.
[4] Overbeck, *op. cit.* 332.
[5] *Ibid.* 371.

Apollo of Kanachos[1] which was erected at Miletus, carried off by the Persians, and subsequently restored by Seleukos. A vase in Munich by the artist of the Foundry Vase shows on one side Athena inspecting a small figure of a horse.[2] This is usually assumed to be the Wooden Horse of Troy, but it has been rightly pointed out by Lehmann-Hartleben that this representation does not agree with the usual illustration of that tale,[3] and, further, the horse is small. Thus the horse may be a wooden model for casting a horse in bronze. There is thus some other evidence for Kluge's suggestion apart from the results of his technical examination of early bronzes. Kluge[4] too links this new technical process of hollow casting large size bronze figures with the names of Rhoikos and Theodoros and so accepts the tradition preserved by Pausanias and Diodorus. It must be remembered that only the adoption of a process of hollow casting would have made

1 Overbeck, *op. cit.* 403, 404.

2 Beazley, *op. cit.* p. 187, 3; *J.d.I.* 1929, p. 25, fig. 15.

3 *J.d.I.* 1929, p. 26, note 4.

4 *Ibid.* p. 28 ff.

large size bronze statues economically possible. De Ridder[1] has put together some valuable observations on the cost of making full size bronze statues and these, even when hollow cast, were expensive. They were, however, comparatively easy to transport as shown by the statues which Xerxes carried off to Persia. Marble figures, on the other hand, were comparatively cheap as far as material was concerned, but carving was not cheap and the cost of transport, especially land transport, for large blocks of marble was always high.[2] The wrecked cargoes of Hellenistic or later times of Antikythera[3] and Mahdia[4] show that bronzes and marbles were then being transported by sea without any apparent difficulty, but we have no indication whatsoever of the cost of such carriage at that date.

At any rate a brief survey of the records, both literary and monumental, is enough to show that down to the middle of the sixth

[1] *Rev. Arch.* II, 1915, p. 97 ff.

[2] Schweitzer, *Neue Heidelberger Jahrbücher*, 1925, p. 47 ff.

[3] Svoronos, *Athener Nationalmuseum*, I, p. 1 ff., pls. V–XX.

[4] *Mon. Piot.* XVII, p. 29 ff.; XVIII, p. 5 ff.

century, that is to say, to the period of Rhoikos and Theodoros, the principal materials for monumental sculpture in Greece were stone or marble, though the probability that wood was also used must be taken into account.[1] From then to the age of Praxiteles in the fourth century bronze was the main material for monumental sculptures. This general statement excludes for the time architectural sculpture which from the nature of things would be in stone or marble. Further, in the fifth century the favourite materials for large cult statues were gold and ivory, but, as already pointed out, these are examples of metal chasing which is closely connected with bronze working.[2] It is possible that we can see a reflection of this preference for stone or marble in the archaic period, for bronze in the mature age, and for a revival of stone or marble from the

[1] Terracotta was probably also used in some cases for cult statues.

[2] An acrolithic cult statue of marble and bronze, such as that of Apollo Alaios (Orsi, *Templum Apollinis Alaei*, p. 135 ff.), would presumably have been a cheaper substitute for one in ivory and gold.

time of Praxiteles onwards, in the results of excavation at great sanctuaries, Olympia, Delphi, Delos, the Acropolis. At these sanctuaries the large bronzes found (and with these one can class the inscribed bases for bronze statues now lost) fall largely within the period from 510 to 350 B.C. The marble statues, on the other hand, apart from the architectural sculpture, are archaic and on the Acropolis do not come below 480 B.C. for the most part, or are of fourth century or later date like the Thessalian group at Delphi and the marble warrior of Pergamene style from Delos. There is one notable exception, the Nike of Paionios, but to this we will return later. This is, of course, a generalisation, and to a generalisation there are always exceptions, but other evidence can be cited in support. There are the archaic marble sculptures from the Ptoion, the Heraion at Samos, and the temple of Branchidai. In the National Museum at Athens the marble sculptures, which can be presumed to be originals, excluding stelai and architectural work, are either archaic or else fourth century or later.

As bronze sculpture grew in popularity at the end of the sixth century and it was observed that bronze gave greater movement to the figure and consequently greater naturalism, it would follow almost inevitably that the bronze technique would exercise its influence on marble and stone sculpture which thus in its turn would tend to greater naturalism. 'The brass that seems to speak' would have inspired 'the stone that breathes and struggles'. Whether marble sculpture would have abandoned the tradition of frontality without the stimulus of bronze cannot here be discussed. Whether naturalism was or was not the ideal of ancient art is also not immediately pertinent, but ancient critics praised highly works of art which seemed to them at least most natural. The Heifer of Myron is perhaps the best example,[1] but many others could be quoted.

It is thus not surprising that the naturalistic effect of the bronze technique on marble sculpture should be already visible by the close of

[1] Overbeck, *Schriftquellen*, 550–591.

the sixth century. The marble Kore attributed to Antenor (probably wrongly for he was a bronze worker), and the pedimental figures from the Alcmaeonid temple at Delphi, show some traces of the influence of bronze, and it is also observable in the pedimental figures of the Pisistratid Hekatompedon. The pedimental sculptures of the temple of Aphaia in Aegina which date early in the fifth century have a distinctly metallic appearance which is heightened by the small scale of the figures, the tight hard surface of the flesh, and the sharp contours of the heads and their details. Indeed, the marble heads of the Aeginetan pediments find a bronze parallel in the warrior head from the Acropolis,[1] even though, as Kluge suggests, it was made from a wooden model. Another marble with similar characteristics is the torso from Daphni.[2] Such sculptures imitate, of course, not the wooden model for the bronze, but the appearance of the cast bronze after it had been finished off. Aegina was famous as

[1] 'Εφ. 'Αρχ. 1887, pl. 3.

[2] Buschor-Hamann, *Skulpturen d. Zeustempels*, fig. 8.

the centre of an early school of bronze workers and her marble carvers might naturally have imitated the effects achieved by their fellow craftsmen in bronze.

Another case of marble imitating bronze is the Strangford Apollo[1] which falls late, about 500 B.C., in the series of archaic stone or marble kouroi. The advance in naturalism which it shows in contrast to earlier kouroi can be explained by comparing it with the bronze Piombino Apollo.[2]

Another form of art which could equally influence marble sculpture is modelling, and here we recall that, according to Pliny,[3] Pasiteles declared that modelling was the mother of the other three arts, bronze casting, marble carving, and metal chasing. According to one tradition Butades[4] of Sicyon, another home of bronze sculptors, invented modelling in clay. The making of plaster casts from living

[1] *B.M. Cat. Sculpture*, I, I, B 475, pl. xliii; *Met. Mus. Studies*, v, p. 42.

[2] Langlotz, *op. cit.* pls. I, 19.

[3] *N.H.* xxxv, 156.

[4] Pliny, *N.H.* xxxv, 151.

models is attributed to Lysistratos,[1] the brother of Lysippos, in the fourth century, and he is also credited with realism in portraiture in contrast to the idealism of earlier artists. This is only to be expected in an artist who took casts from living models. Pliny adds that he first made casts of bronze statues and that the practice (presumably that of making models and casts) reached such a pitch that thereafter no bronze or marble statues were made without clay models.[2] If Lysistratos took casts of living models and bronze statues, he very likely did so in order that marble copies could be made anywhere with the help of casts from his

[1] Pliny, *N.H.* xxxv, 153.

[2] Overbeck and Welcker take this statement of Pliny as referring to Lysistratos and not to Butades which involves a transposition of the text, as Brunn suggested, who was followed by Münzer and Schweitzer. Butades is said to be the inventor of modelling and casting antefixes and other architectural ornaments in clay. Lysistratos improved the process by taking casts of living models and presumably piece moulds of antique bronzes. See Brunn, *Geschichte d. gr. Künstler*, I, p. 403; Münzer, *Hermes*, xxx, p. 510; Overbeck, *Geschichte d. gr. Plastik*, II, p. 166 f. (he cites Welcker in his note); Reinach, *Rev. Arch.* XLI, 1902, p. 5 ff.; Schweitzer, *Xenokrates von Athen*, p. 48.

moulds. He may, indeed, have been one of the first to supply the market with marble copies from antique bronzes. The marble Diadumenos from Delos,[1] after Polykleitos' bronze, a copy which presumably must date before 80 B.C., would probably have been made by pointing either direct from the original or from a plaster cast of it. The latter is quite possible because plaster moulds for making casts of antique bronzes exist. There is part of a piece mould for casting a figure in the style of Polykleitos in Cairo[2] and, in any case, the Delian Diadumenos is later in date than the period of Lysistratos. Another marble copy of a Polykleitan bronze, the Lansdowne Amazon, now in the Metropolitan Museum, New York, shows quite clearly on the top of the head the mark of a point.[3] At all events Pliny's statement that the practice reached such a pitch that thereafter no bronze or marble statue was made without a clay model deserves close

[1] Richter, *op. cit.* fig. 650.

[2] *Cat. Gén. d. Ant. Ég. du Musée du Caire*, Edgar, *Greek Moulds*, No. 32336, pl. i.

[3] *Met. Mus. Bulletin*, XXX, 1935, p. 67.

attention. It would[1] mean that at least from the time of Lysippos onwards every sculptor working in marble or bronze made a clay model first. Bronzes would be cast after the clay model,[2] and the marbles would be measured and pointed off exactly in the fashion which has persisted to our own day. That is to say, sculptors according to Michelangelo's definition would have been not true sculptors, but modellers. This use of models finds other echoes. Artists paid higher prices for models by Arkesilaos than for finished work of others.[3] This is quite natural, for the clay models would have been originals from his own hand while the finished works of others would have been bronzes cast by bronze founders or marbles carved by pupils or stone masons. The works of the school of Pasiteles[4] are marbles, and thus

[1] If Brunn is correct the practice would have been still older, for though Butades' date is not known, he certainly preceded Lysistratos.

[2] See Pliny's account of the model for Zenodoros' colossal Nero, *N.H.* xxxiv, 46.

[3] Pliny, *N.H.* xxxv, 155.

[4] Laurence, *Classical Sculpture*, p. 66 f.

presumably would also have been pointed off from clay models.

It is, however, possible, I think, to trace the use of models even further back. There is the well-known passage in the Epidaurus inscription which mentions a payment made to Timotheos the artist for τύποι which were almost certainly clay models on a small scale for the pedimental groups of the temple of Asklepios.[1] This confirms the fourth century use of models.[2]

In the fifth century two competitions are mentioned. The first is the Amazon competition[3] in which Pheidias, Kresilas, Polykleitos, and Phradmon took part. To judge by the marble copies we possess the Amazons were in bronze and the artists mentioned were certainly bronze workers. Now no artist entering

[1] Neugebauer, *J.d.I.* 1926, p. 82 ff.

[2] The identity of Chalcosthenes, a modeller according to Pliny (*N.H.* xxxv, 155), with Kaikosthenes, a late fourth-century sculptor, is not certain, Löwy, *I.G.B.* 113–117, cf. *ibid.* 220.

[3] Pliny, *N.H.* xxxiv, 53; Furtwängler, *Masterpieces*, p. 128 ff.; Pfuhl, *J.d.I.* 1926, p. 1 ff.

a competition would go to the great expense of sending in a full size figure in bronze. As has always been done in such competitions in more recent times, he would submit a model in clay or some similar plastic material. The other competition is that between Alkamenes and Agorakritos[1] for an Aphrodite which was won by the former. The latter sold his statue on the condition that it should not be set up in Athens. It was bought by the people of Rhamnus, converted into a statue of Nemesis and erected there. This statue was in marble and a surviving fragment of it is in the British Museum.[2] Here again the artists would have submitted models for the competition, and it stands to reason that the alteration of Agorakritos' figure from an Aphrodite into a Nemesis would hardly have been feasible unless he had first submitted only a plastic model. Paionios of Mende won the prize in the competition for making the akroteria for the Zeus temple at Olympia.[3] These were figures of Nike and

[1] Pliny, *N.H.* XXXVI, 17. [2] Richter, *op. cit.* fig. 633.
[3] Löwy, *I.G.B.* 49.

cauldrons which were gilt and therefore presumably of bronze.[1] Here again it can hardly be imagined that the artist would submit completely finished figures, but only clay or wax models. Further, the famous Nike of Paionios at Olympia[2] which is in marble shows in its composition all the characteristics of a model built up in clay. Pomtow[3] has suggested that it was the marble replica of a bronze dedicated by the Messenians at Delphi on a similar triangular base. If this can be accepted we could see in the lost bronze at Delphi and in the Olympia marble, copies in different materials made after a clay or wax model by Paionios. This possibility is strengthened by the fact that two marble replicas of the head of the Nike have been recognised.[4] In view of the difficulty of making reasonably accurate copies of the

[1] Pausanias, v, 10, 4.

[2] *Olympia*, III, p. 182 ff., pls. xlvi–xlviii.

[3] *J.d.I.* 1922, p. 55 ff. The objections to Pomtow's suggestion on chronological grounds are not valid, because the later date for the Nike is now generally accepted, see Pfuhl, *J.d.I.* 1926, pp. 25, 159 ff.; Richter, *op. cit.* p. 241 ff.

[4] *Olympia*, III, p. 188 ff., fig. 222; Richter, *op. cit.* figs. 639–641.

head of the marble Nike at Olympia when she stood aloft on her tall pedestal (over nine metres high) one can only imagine that a model of it was accessible. Wax models were supplied for some of the ceiling ornaments of the Erechtheum.[1] Again, a number of masons (not one of whom is recorded anywhere among the names of ancient artists that have come down to us) were employed to carve the figures for the frieze of the same building.[2] It can hardly be supposed that the carvers of the figures made their own designs, but that they presumably copied in marble the designs of some artist who had designed the frieze as a whole. Thus it is legitimate to assume that behind the figures of the Erechtheum frieze stand the models, clay or wax, of some artist who had been invited by the authorities to design them. Carpenter sees in the frieze of the balustrade of the temple of Nike the hands of six masters who carved it.[3] This conclusion seems quite acceptable, but

[1] *Erechtheum*, p. 409.

[2] *Erechtheum*, pp. 405 ff., 413 ff.

[3] *Sculpture of the Nike Temple Parapet; A.J.A.* 1929, p. 467 ff.

they should probably not be called masters. The Athenians would hardly have assigned six separate sections of a homogeneous frieze to six different artists to work as they pleased. A definite design was surely composed and planned for the balustrade by some one artist. No one looking at the frieze as recomposed to-day can imagine that it is the work of six different brains. The nature of the composition, coherent and symmetrical Carpenter calls it,[1] forbids us to envisage any other possibility than that of a single artist as designer of the whole frieze. Once the design was composed and approved, then it would be quite reasonable to entrust the carving of the six different sections to six different stone carvers. These would not have been masters but carvers like those who carved the figures for the frieze of the Erechtheum. The more the subject is considered the more is it evident that, for compositions like the friezes of the Nike temple and the Erechtheum, designs and models by some competent artist must have been sup-

[1] *Op. cit.* p. 77.

plied and that these were later translated into marble on the scale required by professional carvers, no doubt under the eye of the designer. Blümel has recognised that the pediment groups of the Zeus temple at Olympia, which date about 450 B.C., were pointed off from models,[1] for in several cases the points are still extremely obvious. Study of these pediments shows that they are definitely plastic.[2] The figures were obviously designed to be translated into marble, for the outstanding limbs of marble are provided with natural supports.[3] The figures are weighted with masses of marble at the feet to protect the ankles, the weak spot of a male statue in marble, and to give weight to enable them to stand in the pediments. The figures were, of course, fastened with clamps to the wall behind them, but they were

[1] *Griechische Bildhauerarbeit*, p. 29 ff., pls. 14, 15.

[2] A vase in Berlin which is dated about 470–460 B.C. bears a scene showing Athena modelling a horse, presumably in clay; Richter, *op. cit.* fig. 431; Furtwängler-Reichhold, III, pl. 162.

[3] For instance the group N.O. of the west pediment, *Olympia*, III, pl. XXVI.

naturally far safer if they could stand upright by themselves without undue risk of overbalancing.

For the Parthenon pediments, too, models were probably provided. The accounts[1] show that in the years 438–437 and 437–436 the overseers were selling surplus gold and ivory left over from the construction of the Parthenos. It was probably then that accusations of dishonesty were raised against Pheidias.[2] The sale of public property under such circumstances could easily give rise to accusations of fraud. One of the tales against Pheidias, who is usually described in his relation to the Parthenos as ἐργολάβος, contractor,[3] was that he had sold some of the ivory for his own benefit. At any rate on his accusation Pheidias went to Elis and there, according to one authority, he

[1] *A.J.A.* 1913, p. 78 ff.; 1921, p. 243 ff.

[2] Overbeck, *Schriftquellen*, 627–632.

[3] The status of a popular artist in Greece was not as high as that of a favourite artist to-day. Sculptors, either in bronze or marble, were on the whole rather low in the social scale. The mention of Pheidias as a friend of Pericles is an exception. Schweitzer has recently treated the subject very fully, *Neue Heidelberger Jahrbücher*, 1925, p. 28 ff.

is said to have died. The pediment groups for the Parthenon were begun according to the accounts in 439–438 and for the year 434–433 is recorded the payment of a large sum to the sculptors. Though the inscription is damaged the word sculptors is certain. So probably, just as in the case of the Erechtheum, several men were employed to carve the pedimental figures of the Parthenon. If so, they must have carved from models. There are in existence small size marble versions of several of the figures of the west pediment of the Parthenon which were found in excavations at Eleusis.[1] They are about one-third of the full size. Furtwängler[2] long ago thought that they were of fifth century date and might have come from Pheidias' studio. Carpenter[3] independently, because he does not mention Furtwängler's opinion, considers them to be of the fourth century and has shown their importance for reconstructing the pediment. These small marble figures may well be marble versions

[1] 'Εφ. 'Αρχ. 1890, p. 219 ff., pls. 12, 13.

[2] *Statuenkopieen im Altertum*, p. 6. [3] *Hesperia*, I, p. 11 ff.

of the original clay or wax models on the same scale as the wax models themselves. One-third of the final size intended would be a reasonable scale for a model and for a carver copying would be an easy scale to work from in making full size figures. Whatever view we take of these models, though the explanation just given seems sound, the fatal plural in the inscription and the strong probability that Pheidias was then in Elis[1] seem to make it reasonable to suppose that Pheidias can never have taken a direct hand in carving the pediments of the Parthenon. For one man single-handed to carve the whole of two pediments like those of the Parthenon would be a colossal task. The mere physical labour would be overwhelming. Thus Pheidias may have designed the Parthenon pediments, though all authorities are silent on this point, but in view of the evidence the most we can say is not that they are *by* Pheidias, but *after* him or in his style. Examination of the top of the head of the

[1] The arguments that the Zeus was later than the Parthenos seem to me convincing, see Richter, *op. cit.* p. 220 ff.

Theseus of the east pediment of the Parthenon shows in the middle of the head slightly forward of the actual crown a curiously flattened space among the hair which is badly weathered. This flattening is rather smooth and so presumably not caused by weathering. It gives the appearance of a point which has been chiselled off, but not worked over, and suggests the point on the Lapith head[1] in the west pediment at Olympia. It is about roughly square and about 1½ inches across, a size which would be very suitable for a point. The top of the head of the Theseus apparently came close to the cornice of the pediment and so there would have been no need for it to be carefully worked, for it would never have been visible. Thus there is no immediate objection to considering it a point. Just forward of it nearer the brow is a roughly levelled space rather larger which gives the impression of having been dressed down to fit under the slope of the cornice. This, however, would not explain the smooth place first described.

[1] Blümel, *op. cit.* pl. 14 b.

If it is a point it is practically decisive evidence for the pedimental figures of the Parthenon having been pointed off from models as suggested. In any case till the top of the head can be cleaned and carefully studied no definite pronouncement can be made.

Models in clay and plaster were presumably familiar to Pheidias. The great cult statue of Zeus at Megara designed by Theokosmos who had worked with Pheidias was never finished. The head was completed in gold and ivory but the rest as seen by Pausanias[1] was in clay and plaster, presumably the full size model for those parts of the figure. Behind the temple were half-worked pieces of wood which Pausanias says Theokosmos was to cover with gold and ivory to complete the statue. This seems to show that the clay and plaster parts were not intended to be covered with gold and ivory, but were the model for a wooden framework to be covered with those materials. If Theokosmos used this method presumably it was not unknown to his contemporary Pheidias,

[1] I, 40, 4.

who was the great master for making gold and ivory cult statues.

Thus the evidence available all seems to indicate that by the middle of the fifth century at least artists made models for any important piece of work especially for architectural sculpture. In the metopes of the Parthenon at least three styles can be distinguished. This does not necessarily mean that more than one designer was employed for the metopes but only that more than one carver was employed to execute them. Similarly with monuments of which something survives, such as the Mausoleion, and the temple of Athena Alea at Tegea, we can hardly now imagine that the ancient authorities in saying that their decoration was the work of Skopas, Bryaxis, Leochares, and Timotheos[1] meant that those artists executed the carving of the friezes and pedimental sculptures all themselves, but only that they designed them. It would seem, therefore, to be more correct to speak of the fragments from Tegea as *after* Skopas and of a frieze of the Mausoleion

[1] Richter, *op. cit.* p. 267 ff.

as *after* Timotheos. In the case of this last artist we know that he supplied models for the pediments at Epidaurus which similarly must be described as *after* and not *by* Timotheos. It would be extremely unwise to consider the handling of the marble of the Epidaurus figures as a hall mark of Timotheos or that of the Tegea fragments as the characteristic manner of Skopas. What we can attribute with safety to these artists is the design but not the execution. The treatment of the surface, the tools used, and other details would depend on the stone cutters employed and only design and composition would depend on the artists, who presumably supervised the whole. Thus we shall apparently be wiser to estimate marble sculpture executed after the coming into favour of bronze not by its bodily surface and the manner in which that is carved, but rather by the purpose and spirit of the whole. It stands to reason, too, that the Aeginetan pediments, where Webster[1] discerns three sculptors 'not divided by pediments', and the archaic architectural

[1] *J.H.S.* 1931, p. 183.

sculptures which precede them in date must have been designed before they were executed, though what form the designs took we cannot now say. The decoration of the Siphnian treasury at Delphi too must have been designed by some one artist. The pediments of the Alcmaeonid temple at Delphi and those of the Pisistratid Hekatompedon must also have been executed from designs specially made for the purpose by some artist. Neither of these works can reasonably have been executed by one carver alone. If the design is that of one man, then the execution would have to be attributed to a group of carvers such as those who worked the Erechtheum frieze. Thus for architectural sculpture at least and for all large sculptural groups the artist is in much the same relation to the finished work as the architect. As regards bronzes, too, the evidence of the Foundry Vase at Berlin shows that several workmen were employed to fit together and finish off a bronze statue after it was cast. So here again the final state of a statue was not due to the artist alone and unaided.

Do these considerations help at all with one question now hotly debated, that of the Hermes of Praxiteles?[1] From its first discovery till recently this was universally regarded as an undoubted original from the master's own hand. In view of the practical certainty that by the time of Praxiteles in the fourth century models in clay or wax were fairly commonly used, this judgment should be reconsidered. When such models are employed it usually follows that the finished marble, as in the case of Rodin's work, was not necessarily executed by the artist himself but by professional stone cutters or perhaps by pupils. In fact, as often in more modern times, a sculptor who makes use of clay models as a rule does not carve much, if any, of the finished marble himself. As has been pointed out by Miss Richter,[2] the general composition of other works of Praxiteles, the Satyr, the Aphrodite of Knidos, the Apollo Sauroktonos, shows at once that the

[1] See *A.J.A.* 1931, p. 249 ff.; *Antiquity*, June 1934, p. 151 ff.

[2] *A.J.A.* 1931, p. 280 ff.

support, a tree trunk, drapery, or whatever it may be, is not merely an integral but an essential part of the design. Praxiteles is the first of the great artists after the sixth century who was universally famous as a worker in marble. He may have realised the great possibilities of marble as the most satisfactory medium for rendering the flesh of his smooth, soft, rather sensuous figures. Up to his time bronze was the favourite material for every leading sculptor and models of some material were essential for bronze. A nude or semi-nude male figure in marble is by itself apt to be top heavy and, as already stated, the marble legs have a tendency to snap at the ankle unless supported. Consequently in the Delian copy of the Polykleitan bronze Diadumenos a tree trunk is added behind one leg to support it and to give more weight at the base and so give the figure greater stability. Praxiteles worked in bronze also. If he, like Rodin, planned to have the models for his bronzes also worked in marble he would have realised at once that some form of support was inevitable. I would suggest therefore that in composing his statues he deliberately made the support an essential part of the design so that the figure could be executed either in bronze or in marble without any great alteration. Rodin's Prodigal Son in bronze has no support behind, but one at least of the marble versions of it has a marble support behind.[1] This support has, however, no meaning and is a clumsy technical device such as can be seen in most of the Graeco-Roman copies of antique bronzes, though in many cases the copyist attempted to give a purpose to the support by hanging something on it, a quiver and bow in the case of the Delian Diadumenos. Praxiteles, however, with his mind set on the ultimate design of the whole, whatever the material, gave from the first a definite purpose to the support which he knew was otherwise otiose and tiresome. In the Hermes the support is an essential part of the whole composition. No human figure could stand by itself with such a weight on its left

[1] See the supports on the Diadumenos in New York, *A.J.A.* 1935, p. 50, fig. 6.

arm unless there were a support on the left side for it to lean upon. The main objections to the Hermes which first suggested it might be a copy are the unfinished back, the bronze treatment of the hair, and the short piece of marble connecting the left leg with the support. If we could imagine that Praxiteles designed a figure able to be cast in bronze or to be worked in marble these difficulties would at once vanish. I would suggest therefore that the Hermes is a marble version of Praxiteles' composition carved in his studio [1] after a cast of a clay model which he, following what we may perhaps call his normal practice, so designed that it would be a suitable subject either for bronze or for marble. It is possible that there was a bronze

[1] I suggest it is a copy made in the artist's studio because the treatment of the flesh and the handling of the drapery, which, *pace* Professor Carpenter, is far superior to that of the Germanicus, are unrivalled for their brilliance among ancient marble sculpture preserved to us. The Agias in flesh treatment is inferior and only few ancient marbles can approach the Hermes in this respect. Such are the Dying Gaul and the Dresden torso both of which are probably rightly held to be contemporary copies of the models for the bronzes erected at Pergamum.

replica of the Aphrodite at Knidos,[1] but it depends on the exact shade of meaning given to one word in Pliny,[2] who says: *Veneremque quae ipsa aedis (Felicitatis) incendio cremata est Claudii principatu marmoreae illi suae per terras inclutae parem.* If *parem* can here mean counterpart, then we could assume that Praxiteles' famous Aphrodite was executed both in marble, which naturally gave the more striking effect, and in bronze. We can, too, probably recognise a parallel case in the Agias of Lysippos.[3] A bronze which bore the artist's name was erected at Pharsalos and a marble figure unsigned was set up at Delphi. The bronze has perished, but the marble survives and it certainly appears to have been carved by a stone cutter rather than by an artist. If then the bronze at Pharsalos were the original, it can

[1] The back of the Vatican copy shows a rectangular marble stump, Blinkenberg, *Knidia*, p. 124, pl. 2. Blinkenberg calls it a *verschmiertes Loch*, but neither cast nor photograph gives this impression. Can it be the remains of a point?

[2] *N.H.* xxxiv, 69.

[3] Richter, *op. cit.* p. 286 ff.; Johnson, *Lysippos*, p. 123 ff.

well be understood why the artist's name was omitted from the marble version.

It is this pointing off into marble from a clay or wax model which gives the later Greek sculpture in marble a quality different from that of the archaic sculpture. The latter was conceived as stone or marble and executed direct in that material. An artist may reasonably have made some preliminary sketch for his statue, but there was then no pointing off from a model. This direct carving gives to archaic sculpture its perpetual freshness, its spirit of untiring, confident youth. The simplicity of this method in stone or marble, the true method of sculpture, is its great charm, and makes it always satisfying. The bronzes of the fifth and fourth centuries have a natural dignity and serenity, a loftiness of conception which is unapproachable. The marbles of a later day for all their technical perfection and their facile execution have a tendency to academic sophistication which is very pleasant at first sight but rather tires on close acquaintance.

These three phases of Greek sculpture which this approach reveals could be compared with the three masters of Attic drama. The period of archaic marble or stone sculpture recalls the style of Aeschylus, the period of bronze sculpture which was also the age of chryselephantine cult statues that of Sophocles, and the last period when marble and bronze were both alike made freely from models in clay or wax the style of Euripides. It is not for us to say that any one period is better than another. Each period has its admirers, for likes and dislikes are individual and personal. In this approach, however, we tread the path of the Greek critics themselves, and by adopting their own division of the sculptural arts we realise from the considerations just set out that

[1] Mr Seltman has kindly called my attention to an anecdote of Aeschylus in Porphyry (*de abstin.* 2, 18) probably drawn from Theophrastus (see *Aesch. Trag.*, ed. Wilamowitz, pp. 16, 46). Aeschylus when at Delphi is said to have declared that old statues, though simple in workmanship, were superhuman; and, though he marvelled at new statues for their over-elaborate workmanship, yet he considered they had about them less of the superhuman (θείου). See *Camb. Univ. Reporter*, Feb. 20th, 1934.

in sculpture, especially for the two later phases, design and intention rather than mere execution disclose the spirit of the artist. In other words, after the archaic period the artist was an architect who designed and inspired sculpture and not necessarily the actual maker.

For EU product safety concerns, contact us at Calle de José Abascal, 56–1°, 28003 Madrid, Spain or eugpsr@cambridge.org.

www.ingramcontent.com/pod-product-compliance
Ingram Content Group UK Ltd.
Pitfield, Milton Keynes, MK11 3LW, UK
UKHW040723120726
473066UK00028B/247

* 9 7 8 1 1 0 7 6 7 2 1 2 3 *